Solid Seasons

A One-Act Play

by

Stephen Evans

This is a work of fiction. The names, characters, places, and incidents are either the products of the author's imagination or are used fictitiously, and any resemblance to actual persons living or dead, business establishments, events, or locales is entirely coincidental.

For production permissions and rights, contact:

info@TimeBeingMedia.com

Solid Seasons: 1st Edition

ISBN: 978-1-953725-09-7

"There was one other with whom I had "solid seasons," long to be remembered, at his house in the village, and who looked in upon me from time to time."

Henry David Thoreau,

Walden

STEPHEN EVANS

Cast of Characters

Waldo   Ralph Waldo Emerson

Henry   Henry David Thoreau

Setting

Thoreau's cabin at Walden Pond.

Time

July 4th, 1847.

STEPHEN EVANS

ACT I SCENE 1

Setting: Thoreau's cabin.

At Rise: HENRY is at his desk. He is struggling to light an oil lamp.

HENRY
Let there be light.

WALDO knocks and enters.

WALDO
Hello Henry. How are the beans?

HENRY
Welcome Mr. Emerson. Beans?

WALDO
Mrs. Emerson has sent me for some beans.

Pause.

HENRY

Beans.

WALDO

Beans?

Henry nods. This is a game they play, a contest, but beneath the tension between them is only barely hidden.

Waldo thinks.

WALDO
Pounding beans is good to the end of pounding empires one of these days; but if, at the end of years, it is still only beans![1]

HENRY
Ha!

Henry picks up a piece of paper and reads.

HENRY
The same sun which ripens my beans illumines at once a system of earths like ours.[2]

Waldo nods.

WALDO
You.

Henry nods.

WALDO
Is that new?

HENRY
It is. A book I think. Maybe a lecture. But I think it's a book.

WALDO
About?

---

[1] Emerson. *Eulogy of Thoreau*
[2]. Thoreau, *Walden*

HENRY

Me I suppose.

WALDO

You?

HENRY

Yes.

WALDO

You're writing about you?

HENRY

Franklin did it. Rousseau did it.

WALDO

Of course Henry. Of course.

HENRY

Even you have done it, Mr. Emerson.

WALDO

When?

HENRY

In your essay on Experience. You wrote about little Waldo. How you felt when he. When he got sick.

WALDO

Yes. Yes. But. That was to illustrate a point. I wasn't writing about myself.

HENRY

I am doing the same. Just on a slightly larger scale.

WALDO
What point are you illustrating?

HENRY
I'm not sure yet.

WALDO
I see.

HENRY
It's a work in progress.

WALDO
Aren't they all?

HENRY
It's about. My time here.

WALDO
DaVinci said that art is never finished.

HENRY
What I have learned.

WALDO
L'arte non è mai Finita.

HENRY
What?

WALDO
DaVinci. That's what he said. I thought you
knew Italian, Henry.

HENRY
Italian? Yes. A bit. French. Latin. Spanish.
German. Greek.

WALDO
And your English is coming along well too.

HENRY
Is it? Praise from Ralph Waldo Emerson
himself. What more could one ask?

WALDO
You have so much promise Henry. I don't
want you to waste it.

Henry holds up a sheaf of papers.

HENRY
I am transforming my journal into a book.

Waldo smiles.

WALDO
Now where did you learn that?

HENRY
I wonder.

*Henry puts down the papers, looks
around the cabin.*

HENRY
I'm thinking of calling it Life in the Woods.

WALDO
These are hardly the woods, Henry.

Henry smiles.

HENRY
It is a domestic wilderness.

WALDO

Henry, you know I dislike it when you do that. It is a rhetorical trick of which you are much too fond.

Henry smiles more broadly.

HENRY

I know.

Now Waldo smiles.

WALDO

Ha. Anyway, you're a mile from the town common.

Henry pauses. Back to the game.

HENRY

Common.

Waldo takes his time. Then.

WALDO

Nothing astonishes men so much as common sense and plain dealing.[3]

Henry picks up his sheath of papers again.

HENRY

If one advances confidently in the direction of his dreams, and endeavors to live the life

---

[3] Emerson, *Art*

which he has imagined, he will meet with a success unexpected in common hours.[4]

They pause.

Waldo nods.

WALDO
You again.

HENRY
Yours was good though.

WALDO
Thank you. I'll have to try and remember it.

Waldo takes the sheath of papers from Henry.

He peruses them.

Mumbling.

Nodding.

Scowling.

Henry gets nervous.

HENRY
The town common is a mile and three quarters.

WALDO
(Not looking up)

---

[4] Thoreau, *Walden*

You are the surveyor. I bow to your superior knowledge.

(*Now he looks up*)
As to distance.

Henry smiles.

HENRY
You don't like the title Life in the Woods?

WALDO
Simple titles, Henry. One word if possible. Nature. Experience. Self-Reliance.

HENRY
That's two words.

WALDO
It's hyphenated. Counts as one.

HENRY
I bow to your superior knowledge. As to hyphens.

Waldo sits and glances around the cabin.

WALDO
Anyway, why are you working on something new? I thought you were still reworking the other one. The river book.

HENRY
A Week on the Concord and Merrimack Rivers.

WALDO
Short titles, Henry. Short titles.

WALDO

I'll try to remember, Mr. Emerson.

WALDO

And three names. If you have them. Ralph
Waldo Emerson. David Henry Thoreau. It
adds gravity. We all need a little gravity.

HENRY

Henry David. You forget I changed it.

WALDO

Ah yes. Henry David Thoreau. That does
sound better. Perhaps I should have done that.
Waldo Ralph Emerson?

Pause

BOTH

No.

WALDO

When you have Ralph and Waldo to choose
from, I suppose it makes no difference.

HENRY

Emerson has a solid ring to it.

WALDO

Do you think?

HENRY

Oh yes.

WALDO

Perhaps. Perhaps you are just used to it.

HENRY

No one can pronounce Thoreau. They always put the accent on the second syllable.

WALDO

It is better to be famously mispronounced than pronounced infamous.

Henry pauses. Repeats the phrase to himself.

HENRY

That makes no sense.

Waldo pauses. Repeats the phrase to himself.

WALDO

True. It sounds good though.

HENRY

Fame is not something I shall ever know.

WALDO

It was not something I expected when I was a young minister in Boston. But here we are. Though some would say I am more infamous than famous.

HENRY

Ha.

WALDO

First the publication of my little Nature book, which caused so much ruckus. Then my Divinity School disaster.

HENRY

It was a fine speech.

WALDO

Lecture. Politicians give speeches.

HENRY

Sorry.

WALDO

They still won't allow me to speak there.

HENRY

Lecture. See I do listen.

Waldo laughs.

WALDO

Still.

HENRY

They don't know you.

WALDO

That is what fame is. Being widely unknown.

HENRY

That makes sense. I just can't quite figure out why.

WALDO

Fame.

Henry thinks.

HENRY

Rather than love, than money, than fame, give me truth.[5]

WALDO

All the toys that infatuate men, and which they play for,--houses, land, money, luxury, power, fame, are the selfsame thing, with a new gauze or two of illusion overlaid. [6]

They pause, thinking.

HENRY

You.

WALDO

I don't know. Yours has a power mine lacks, a straightforwardness. It reminds me of the way I used to write.

HENRY

A young man's phrase, you're saying. You think I will grow out of it?

WALDO

I hope not. I would write that way still if I could. If I still had that confidence. That clarity.

Waldo picks up a paper on the desk.

WALDO

Your essay on Carlyle? It was published?

---

[5] Thoreau, *Walden*
[66] Emerson, *Fate*

HENRY

It was. Though Mr. Greely is having trouble getting me paid for it.

WALDO

Lectures, Henry. That is what the public wants. And you get paid in advance.

HENRY

You do.

WALDO

Your lecture on Mr. Carlyle was well received. Many of our friends remarked on it.

HENRY

I don't think lecturing is for me.

WALDO

Why not?

HENRY

I can't say what I think.

WALDO

Since when? I have never known you to hold back your opinions. On anything.

Henry nods, and smiles.

HENRY

We have that in common.

WALDO

I suppose we do.

HENRY

People don't like me.

WALDO

Everyone likes you Henry. It's just.

HENRY

Yes?

WALDO

They don't understand you. You read all these languages, you are a fine poet, and the best surveyor in Massachusetts, yet you made pencils for a living.

HENRY

Those pencils were an excellent design. I made many improvements. I will stack my pencils up against any.

WALDO

This is what I'm saying Henry. Anything you do you do well. And yet what you do is. Well. People don't understand it.

HENRY

I don't need them to.

WALDO

And now this. Moving here. Building your cabin. It makes no sense to anyone.

HENRY

Channing approves.

WALDO

Don't tell me you are taking advice from him. Channing is simply happy he isn't considered the oddest person in Concord anymore.

HENRY

Is that what I am?

WALDO

Yes, Henry. Yes, you are without doubt the oddest person in a community of very odd people. Channing. Bronson Alcott. His daughter Louisa.

HENRY

Your Aunt Mary.

WALDO

I beg your pardon! Alright, yes. Though I would prefer for her the term exceptional.

HENRY

I would agree.

WALDO

Hawthorne is very odd.

HENRY

Odd? Is that the right word for him?

WALDO

Peculiar?

HENRY

Uncanny?

WALDO

Bizarre?

HENRY

Curious?

WALDO

Weird?

They pause.

TOGETHER

Weird.

HENRY

He is from Salem. They are all weird there.

WALDO

His wife Sophia[7] is from Salem also.

HENRY

Well. Perhaps not all.

WALDO

Another exceptional.

HENRY

Jones Very.

WALDO

He is not from here.

HENRY

He is of here.

WALDO

True. Poor Jones Very.

HENRY

Too much prophesy in his poetry.

---

[7] Pronounced with a long I

WALDO

And yet the sanest mad man I ever met.

HENRY

Harvard will do that to you. Speaking of,
Willie Goodwin.

WALDO

You think? I have some hopes for him.

HENRY

And then of course there is you.

WALDO

Me? I am not odd.

HENRY

Ha!

WALDO

I am not. I am normal. I am average. I simply
think and read and write more than other
people.

HENRY

You think that is not odd?

WALDO

I am the opposite of odd. With me it is simply
too much normal. Which is why I attract so
many odd people. They find me, like opposite
poles.

HENRY

Like gravity. We all circle around you, but
never approach, lest we burn up in the fire of
your mind.

WALDO
Hardly. It sounds good though.

HENRY
Is that why I came to you?

WALDO
I couldn't say. Could you?

Henry is silent for a moment.

HENRY
You never told me what you thought of it.

WALDO
Thought of what?

HENRY
My essay on Carlyle.

WALDO
Ah. Well done. I said so.

HENRY
Exactly. You shook my hand. You said I did
well. But you never said what you thought.

WALDO
That is unusual for me.

HENRY
One might even say odd.

WALDO
One might. Well, it is difficult for me to judge.
You know only the words. I know the man.

HENRY

Does that make a difference? It was his words I was writing about.

WALDO

It is hard for me to be objective.

HENRY

Why?

WALDO

The man is a friend.

HENRY

You can't be objective because he is a friend?

WALDO

I don't know.

HENRY

Are you objective with me?

WALDO

It is not the same.

HENRY

You have no trouble criticizing me. You and Margaret Fuller made something of a sport of it.

WALDO

The pieces you sent to the Dial, they, we, wanted to help. We see so much promise in you Henry.

HENRY

You keep saying that. Of course I know that, Mr. Emerson. I am grateful, to you and to Miss Fuller.

WALDO

We want to see the remarkable abilities we know you possess reach fullness. Maturity.

HENRY

As do I. Why do you think I came out here?

WALDO

I haven't the slightest idea.

HENRY

Don't you?

WALDO

Didn't you like staying with us Henry?

HENRY

Of course I did. You know I did.

WALDO

I thought you did. Everything was in its right place. Everything worked.

HENRY

For you.

WALDO

But not for you?

HENRY

It was not my place. It was not my home. It was not my. Family.

WALDO

We all cared for you Henry. The children.
Mrs. Emerson.

HENRY

I know. I.

*Henry stops. He is getting into dangerous
territory.*

HENRY

So? What did you think of my lecture?

WALDO

I wish you had left me out of it.

HENRY

How? How can I leave you out of anything.
You are Ralph Waldo Emerson.

WALDO

The man who is banished forever from
Harvard Divinity School.

HENRY

The American Plato.

WALDO

The man who is foolish enough to spend his
life writing, and thinking. Usually in that
order.

HENRY

The successor to Montaigne. The genius of
Concord.

Henry pauses.

HENRY

Genius.

WALDO

In every work of genius we recognize our own rejected thoughts.[8]

HENRY

You're quoting yourself.

WALDO

It's hard not to.

HENRY

It breaks the rules.

WALDO

Were there rules?

Henry stares.

WALDO

Fine.

Waldo stares back, discerning.

WALDO

At first glance he measured his companion, and, though insensible to some fine traits of culture, could very well report his weight and caliber. And this made the impression of genius which his conversation sometimes gave.[9]

---

[8] Emerson, Self-Reliance
[9] Emerson, *Tribute* to Thoreau, Atlantic Magazine, 1862

HENRY

It takes a man of genius to travel in his own country, in his native village; to make any progress between his door and his gate.[10]

Waldo shakes his head, tired of the game.

WALDO

I cannot judge.

HENRY

You cannot not. You are everywhere for me. Except here. In this cabin.

WALDO

Except that I am here.

HENRY

But at least I am also here. I am myself here. This is my place. This pond is my pond. These beans are my beans. And I am finding my way here. To something different.

WALDO

Different from me you mean.

HENRY

There is only one Ralph Waldo Emerson.

Long pause.

WALDO

How are the beans this year?

---

[10] Thoreau, Journal 1851

HENRY

The late freeze took the crop. Until then I expected 12 bushels.

WALDO

Fertilizer?

HENRY

None. Except the mold left over from the stumps when I pulled them.

WALDO

Economical.

HENRY

Of necessity.

Waldo looks slyly at Henry.

WALDO

Necessity.

Pause.

HENRY

The better part of the man is soon plowed into the soil for compost. By a seeming fate, commonly called necessity, they are employed, as it says in an old book, laying up treasures which moth and rust will corrupt and thieves break through and steal.[11]

---

[11] Thoreau, *Walden*

WALDO

We are sure, that, though we know not how, necessity does comport with liberty, the individual with the world, my polarity with the spirit of the times.[12]

They pause.

HENRY

You.

Waldo nods.

WALDO

Henry.

HENRY

Of necessity.

Waldo walks around the cabin, inspecting.

WALDO

The cabin is holding up well.

HENRY

You have not visited in a while, Mr. Emerson.

WALDO

I didn't wish to disturb your work. You said you were making progress.

---

[12] Emerson, *Fate*

HENRY
I was. I am. I think.

Henry pauses.

WALDO
How much longer do you plan to stay?

HENRY
That is up to you.

WALDO
How do you mean?

HENRY
This is your land.

WALDO
Henry. Please. I don't wish to argue. At least not about that.

HENRY
We are who we are.

WALDO
I came here to tell you. I'm going away.

HENRY
West? South?

WALDO
East. Back to Europe.

HENRY
How long?

WALDO
Six months this time. Possibly longer.

Pause

HENRY

When?

WALDO

September.

HENRY

Impossible. What of your trees sir?

WALDO

My orchard you mean?

HENRY

You may possibly get in your peaches by then, the Early Rose and the Presidents. And your pears may well be fine, the Seckels and the Bloodgoods certainly. But what of your apples? The Gravensteins, the Bellflowers and the Hightops? And the quince. Don't get me started on the quince.

WALDO

I have been very concerned about the quince. You know I love my quince apple pie. Mrs. Emerson's pies are the wonder of New England.

HENRY

I remember.

WALDO

So I thought. I was hoping. We all, the family, you see, were hoping. The orchard has never fared so well as when you were tending it, Henry.

HENRY

No.

WALDO

Your apple needs you Henry. The one you grew, the one we named for you. The Thoreau is wasting away in your absence.

HENRY

I have my work here.

WALDO

I don't understand this choice, Henry. When you asked to build out here, I agreed. But I didn't understand. I still don't.

HENRY

My work is here.

WALDO

You are a talented poet.

HENRY

I'm not a poet. I don't know what I am but it isn't a poet.

WALDO

Then write something else.

HENRY

I'm trying.

WALDO

Solitude is necessary. I understand that. But isolation? For one with your temperament. Is that wise?

Henry pauses.

HENRY

Wisdom.

WALDO

Henry.

HENRY

Wisdom.

WALDO

Can't we?

HENRY

Wisdom.

WALDO

To finish the moment, to find the journey's end in every step of the road, to live the greatest number of good hours, is wisdom.[13]

HENRY

How insufficient is all wisdom without love[14].

Neither speaks for a moment.

WALDO

The children miss you Henry.

---

[13] Emerson, *Experience*
[14] Thoreau, *Journals*

HENRY
I still see them.

WALDO
Mrs. Emerson misses you.

HENRY
I miss them all.

WALDO
Then come home, Henry.

HENRY
It isn't my home. I will never have a home. Not in that sense. Nor wife. Nor children. I know that now. It is not a life meant for me. Or a life I wasn't meant for.

WALDO
You don't have to make that choice. I know there is a pressure. Yes there are compromises. Distractions. Interruptions certainly. From the work we do. But they are necessary. I don't know how to say it. I'm not speaking of love.

HENRY
Don't, sir.

WALDO
A life together. Children. The things they teach you. The foundation they give you.

HENRY
I saw that foundation crumble.

Waldo pauses, sinks into a chair.

HENRY
I loved him too.

WALDO
He was a wondrous child.

HENRY
I saw him suffer just as you did.

WALDO
My deep-eyed boy.

HENRY
I saw him die.

WALDO
My Waldo.

HENRY
The same year.

WALDO
I know.

HENRY
The same year.

WALDO
I'm sorry.

HENRY
The same year as John.

WALDO
Your brother was. We all.

HENRY
Waldo from scarlet fever and John from
lockjaw.

WALDO

I have never left that room. I am still holding him.

HENRY

Five years ago.

WALDO

Is it five?

HENRY

The year your essays were published. I don't know how you managed it. I don't know. How.

WALDO

It's what we do.

HENRY

It is. Yes.

WALDO

It's what we must do.

HENRY

It's what I am doing.

WALDO

Necessity.

HENRY

Necessity.

WALDO

If you say so, Henry. I don't understand, but I do trust.

HENRY

You see what you invite me back to.

WALDO

My boy. Can't you see that...

HENRY

No. It is not that way, with us. That's not who
we are.

WALDO

Are you sure?

HENRY

I have loved.

WALDO

It's not important.

HENRY

I have loved.

WALDO

Yes yes.

HENRY

I still love.

WALDO

Mrs. Emerson.

Henry turns quickly.

HENRY

Sir?

WALDO

Mrs. Emerson. She would.

HENRY

Yes.

WALDO
She wished me to ask.

HENRY
Yes.

WALDO
Mrs. Emerson would like some beans. If there are any left. That is what I came to ask.

HENRY
Really?

WALDO
She would take me to task if I forgot.

HENRY
For.

WALDO
You know Lidian.

HENRY
I know. Mrs. Emerson.

Waldo walks slowly to the door. Stops.

WALDO
Henry?

Henry pauses. Deciding.

HENRY
What I have, I'll bring.

WALDO
I know you will. It's what we do.

Waldo starts to leave again.

WALDO

Henry.

HENRY

Yes, Mr. Emerson?

WALDO

I am not objective.

HENRY

Sir?

WALDO

About you. I am not objective about you.

Henry waits.

WALDO

I believe that I am less objective about you
than any friend I have ever had.

HENRY

I'll keep that in mind, Mr. Emerson.

WALDO

Do please, Mr. Thoreau.

*Waldo walks through the door. Looks
around.*

WALDO

Good spot for a cabin, really. I hope it lasts.

Lights fade.

BLACKOUT
THE END

STEPHEN EVANS

Acknowledgements

The world premiere reading of *Solid Seasons* occurred in July 2023, in Concord, Massachusetts at the Thoreau Society Annual Gathering. I am grateful to the Thoreau Society, which sponsored the event, and to Mr. Brent Ranalli, who read with me.

STEPHEN EVANS

Books by
Stephen Evans

Fiction:

The Marriage of True Minds

Let Me Count the Ways (forthcoming)

The Island of Always

Two Short Novels

Painting Sunsets

The Mind of a Writer and other Fables

Non-Fiction:

A Transcendental Journey

Funny Thing Is: A Guide to Understanding Comedy

The Laughing String: Thoughts on Writing

Task of the Human-Hearted

Liebestraum

Plays:

The Ghost Writer

Spooky Action at a Distance

Tourists

Generations (with Morey Norkin and Michael Gilles)

The Visitation Trilogy (forthcoming)

Verse:

Limerosity

Limerositus

Sonets from the Chesapeke

A Look from Winter

Stephen Evans